I0605390

PORTUGUESE HOUSES WITH HISTORY

ORO Editions
Publishers of Architecture, Art, and Design
Gordon Goff: Publisher

www.oroeditions.com
info@oroeditions.com

Published by ORO Editions

Copyright © 2026 ORO Editions.

All rights reserved. No part of this book may be reproduced, stored in a retrieval system, or transmitted in any form or by any means, including electronic, mechanical, photocopying of microfilming, recording, or otherwise (except that copying permitted by Sections 107 and 108 of the U.S. Copyright Law and except by reviewers for the public press) without written permission from the publisher.

You must not circulate this book in any other binding or cover and you must impose this same condition on any acquirer.

Authors: Felipa Almeida and Ana Anahory
Graphic Design: Pablo Mandel, Micaela Carraro / CircularStudio
ORO Managing Editor: Jake Anderson

Typset in Mrs Eaves

10 9 8 7 6 5 4 3 2 1 First Edition

ISBN: 978-1-961856-66-0

Color Separations and Printing: ORO Editions, Inc.
Printed in China.

International Distribution: www.oroeditions.com/distribution

ORO Editions makes a continuous effort to minimize the overall carbon footprint of its publications. As part of this goal, ORO Editions, in association with Global ReLeaf, arranges to plant trees to replace those used in the manufacturing of the paper produced for its books. Global ReLeaf is an international campaign run by American Forests, one of the world's oldest nonprofit conservation organizations. Global ReLeaf is American Forests' education and action program that helps individuals, organizations, agencies, and corporations improve the local and global environment by planting and caring for trees.

Ana Anahory

Felipa Almeida

PORTUGUESE HOUSES WITH HISTORY

TABLE OF CONTENTS

INTRODUCTION

WE HAD AN INTERIOR DESIGN STUDIO for close to a decade. Amongst many things, this led us to discover a less-trodden Portugal, one where craftsmanship and materials are very characteristic of each location. Our many trips gave us precious knowledge and inspiration that we incorporated into our projects. During our travels, we had the unique opportunity to find and visit many special houses—owned by Portuguese families—houses with stories and beauty that make them unique and unforgettable.

Since we began our studio, Portugal has seen a growth in tourism and many of these houses have been transformed into hotels, vacation rentals, and rural accommodation as it became too expensive to maintain them as family homes. This development has led to a certain loss of the character that made them so unique. Due to the repetitive cleaning of personal objects, they have lost their patina of "memory" that was so prevalent. It is from this loss, and to preserve what we can, that led us to write this book about the places that have resisted this change.

Although we no longer work together, our shared passion for these houses and their one-of-a-kind identity was more than enough to convince us to join forces once more. We carefully photographed each of the properties we found to ensure that there was a visual memory that would not be lost. We want this book to pay homage to a Portuguese way of being and a cultural identity that is disappearing with the homogenization of design, objects, and furniture.

A few criteria guided the selection of houses we include in this collection. The first and most crucial detail is that the homes are still inhabited. It does not have to be by the original family, but it is important that the houses see some sort of daily activity that allows us to sense the soul of those that inhabit when we visit. The houses needed to be furnished with original furniture.

We wished to photograph the houses as they were when we arrived, objects were only moved if required or if too distracting. The idea was that we did not intervene in anyway in their mise en scene. We aimed to only use natural light, or the houses installed lighting, so that we got a true picture of day-to-day existence. From the start we acknowledged that we did not want houses that were too polished or were an idealized version of a home. We wanted "real" houses with people living in them.

We invited Birgit Sfat to be the photographer as the quality of her work and her obvious sensitivity toward her subjects was exactly what we were looking for. Her fresh and neutral look toward these houses was essential when it came to selecting and highlighting the details of Portuguese culture, our visual heritage, and the national collective subconscious that can be found in houses like these.

We then reached out to the historian Filipa Avellar to help us contextualize these houses within a Portuguese aesthetic and architectural tradition. Her experience with the inventory of Architectural Heritage made her the ideal scholar for this project and we were very enthusiastic about her joining us.

We hope this book will help raise awareness to what we feel is most valuable about these homes: heritage is precious—a part of our history—and must be preserved. Almost every day we watch with great sadness as pieces of our identity disappear, in part due to a lack of interest about the real value of these buildings. We hope this book can help counteract this by showing the richness of Portuguese built legacy and motivating its preservation and conservation.

ANA ANAHORY AND FELIPA ALMEIDA

I

Casa do Cipreste

ALL STORIES have a beginning and our story began here, at Casa do Cipreste. Anyone with an interest in Portuguese architecture has almost certainly come across this enigmatic house surrounded by the fresh and dense greenery of the Serra de Sintra. We were enamored by the images of this house we saw in books and in 2022 we made the pilgrimage to its gate for the first time.

Designed by its original owner, the renowned architect Raul Lino (1879–1974) the house was completed in 1914 and has remained in the family since. One can feel the dedication given to every detail of its decoration and how it has escaped the trap of becoming frozen in time. It is, nevertheless, a perfect example of a "traditional" Portuguese house, an idea Raul Lino tried to reinvent it in all his projects.

His influences from time spent in England and Germany are apparent throughout, along with North African elements. Harmony is the dominant feature both aesthetically—in the decoration—and structurally in the balance given to the interior and exterior areas.

The integration of various traditional Portuguese decorative arts in the living space is significant. Tiles, fresco paintings of plant motifs, stained glass, and embroidery play a big part along with more daring details like the mixture of various marble types and tiles with a rich and innovative variety of designs, shapes, and colors. The house was built on top of a quarry, and it was important to Raul Lino to bring the rawness of the rock to the building—significant for his interest in ensuring symbiotic functionality.

Raul Lino's close relationship with nature is felt strongly in the garden. The warmth of the house is further amplified by the vibrant and enchanting garden that offers hidden views of the Sintra Palace, which the architect restored and can be seen lurking through the trees. The kitchen is a charismatic yellow and white checkered tiled room full of charmingly arranged pots and knives that reflect both tradition and practicality—an honest blend of history and simple daily activities.

We could not escape the feeling that those who still inhabit this stunning house take time to show a special care for its legacy and are in awe of the creative originality of their ancestor. This is the magic that has allowed this marvel to remain so well preserved despite its age and use.

CASA DO
CIPRESTE

II

Casa Leal

1857

TO TALK about Casa Leal, a discreet mansion in the Reguengos de Monsaraz region, is synonymous with discussing Manuel Mendes Papança, one of the greatest benefactors of this city in Alentejo. He commissioned its construction in 1857 (date symbolically shown on the entrance gate), with the aim of having it included in a larger project that envisioned this area as an urban epicenter within a sort of agricultural capital of the region.

It is surprising that almost nothing of its design reflects the vernacular architecture that dominates this region. On the contrary, it shows Italian influences, which are evident in the color of the façade, the romantic atmosphere in the loggia, and in the frescoes found on the balcony. It is somewhat exotic amongst the simple, whitewashed smaller houses. This difference is felt also on the details like the Palladian pillars painted in yellow stripes and uniquely beautiful arched shape of the doors and windows.

We were impressed by the ingenuity of having almost all the frames face north. The region is prone to severe high temperatures, and this detail signifies a detailed architectural mind designing the home to reduce heat and keep the interior cool and shaded during the worst of the high sun.

Functionality, eccentricity, and beauty are paired organically and with intelligence to ensure that this is truly an original build.

The tall, ornate doors and richly decorated ceilings reflect strong heritage and detailed craftsmanship that has been well-maintained over time. The soft beige and off-white tones of the walls and doors create an inviting, warm atmosphere that beautifully complements the natural wood accents.
Soft, diffused lights add a nostalgic and slightly melancholic ambiance to this cherished family home filled with memories.

We were enchanted by the blue kitchen, the division that showed most commonality with the traditional design of the region. The collection of ceramic plates from various areas of Portugal—all with similar flower elements—are impeccably arranged on one of the walls. The beautiful, patterned tiles on the fireplace in the kitchen further evoked the feeling of being in a traditional Portuguese home.

III

Quinta de Boamense

LOCATED IN FAMALICÃO, on the outskirts of Porto, Casa da Quinta da Boamense is set in a generous plot of land overlooking a vineyard. When we visited, the view was dressed in the colors of autumn. Made entirely of granite, it stands imposingly amongst a garden filled with wisteria and old Camellias Japonica.

Owned by the same family for over three centuries, it has the characteristic design traits of typical manor houses in Minho. Several generations were born and grew up amongst these walls and the historical and sensitive legacy is felt in every corner that makes this house a home. Whether in the library right near the entrance, where a private collection of ancient books is meticulously archived and labelled, or in the kitchen with thick granite walls, a beautiful old fireplace, a stone oven and old copper and clay pieces.

The house is the result of the addition of a unifying central body from the 1850s to two 17th-century constructions covered in thatch. These works, and those that followed, respected the style and character of this manor house from Minho. Large but with a very human scale, this is a farmhouse with a simplicity that moved us. It is cheerful and bright, with a strong but harmonious color palette that gives it serenity.

Like every home, this one has its unique characteristics, one of which is that it is only lived in when the entire family gathers for special occasions and celebrations, such as Easter or the wine harvest season. In this family tradition, wine production and history play a central role. It was here that Alberto Sampaio (1841–1908), a distinguished Portuguese historian, agronomist, and viticulturist, a pioneer in economic history and rural institutions in Portugal, wrote key works in the field of economic history and legislative development, while the Casa de Boamense's wine earned recognition and prizes in Philadelphia, Paris, and Berlin during the 19th century.

A house of celebration, it becomes a meeting place for the family to come together. One can feel the emotional density that permeates to the decorations, which, though few, all seem to tell a story. Exquisitely, in one of the rooms you can find a curious manuscript with floral motifs that was written to celebrate an engagement party on December 14, 1921, where a Camellia Japonica *Emiliana Alba*.

IV

Quinta das Gaeiras

QUINTA DAS GAEIRAS is built upon the grounds of a former tannery founded in the 18th century by a businessman from Hamburg. Located in a village with the same name, on the outskirts of famous Óbidos in central Portugal, this farm is composed of two houses.

The newest house is referred to as the "new house" by the family who has owned it for centuries and is the first thing that catches the eye when one crosses the entrance gate. It sits imposing, with an ochre-colored faÇade that elegantly fits into the dreamy garden that surrounds it. The garden is filled with boxwoods, ferns, camelias, hydrangeas, dahlias, bird of paradise, and impressive sculptures. One enchanting ceramic seahorse stands out in particular in the magical space. The house was built at the turn of the 19th century and has two floors that feature a variety of interior decorating styles. The entrance hall has a neoclassic feel with plaster moldings decorating the walls, Doric-style columns, and an impressive stone staircase. The large living room is decorated in Empire style with a chandelier from the 1920s. These renovations and decorations were done in 1904 by the famous Raul Lino, the owner of casa Cipreste and Casa Branca. The dining room is inspired by the Renaissance and the two balcony rooms are reminiscent of Moorish art with patterned tile wainscoting combined with strong colors on the walls that hint of Flemish paintings. The roofs are vaulted and painted with blue and white plant designs. This house has generous proportions, a grandeur that can be felt even in the kitchen. This large room is one of the most inspiring and leaves one in awe with its vaulted ceilings, marble staircase, beautiful tiles in different tones of white, stone floors and table, and vibrant light that reflects off the immense white that covers the walls.

Inside the "old house" we find smooth walls and low wooden ceilings on both levels where the various colorful, joyful rooms are located and connected by a long corridor full of ceramic pieces from nearby Caldas da Rainha—one of the most interesting and vibrant centers for ceramics in the country. The library is methodically organized and cataloged, and stepping in is like stepping into a world of fantasy.

V

Casa São Sebastião

IT IS STILL POSSIBLE to find little villages in Portugal that seem to have jumped straight off the pages of a period novel. Alcaide is one such village in the municipality of Fundão. It is here that we find Casa de São Sebastião, a house so special that it fits seamlessly into this dreamlike place. With a long façade painted white and dotted with stone details, it is a junction of two architectural bodies—one from 1858, and a more recent one that was completed at the beginning of the 20th century.

We were immediately struck by its elegant exterior with neo-Gothic windows and the beautiful iron railings. Once inside, we felt we stepped back in time. The interiors are highly influenced by the British arts & crafts movement of the mid-1900s. We were invited to lunch in the dining room with the owners surrounded by the stunning boiserie walls covered in painted fabric with floral designs and a fabulous ceiling, wooden fireplace, and ornate furniture.

On the upper floor, a long corridor that leads to various bedrooms. Some of the bedrooms have charming iron beds and typical Alcobaça *chintz bedspreads and others have sophisticated Art Deco*-style furniture from the 1920s. One room has a cabinet used as a shrine with delicate features.

Throughout, the ceiling heights are generous as are the size of the windows that allow warm light to flood in. The lovely kitchen still has an impressive wood-burning stove and a seductive coziness.

VI

Quinta da Aveleda

A WORLD OF LUSH greenery and fantasy: this is Quinta da Aveleda. A property mostly associated with wine but also an estate that holds many worlds within itself.

Built in the 15th century, it was sold in the 17th century and has been owned by the same family ever since. A house and chapel addition were added on in 1671 as shown in the construction date on the façade. In 1910, the house was restored, the exterior now covered in ivy with windows and doors framed in stone.

The landscape frames the home in nature. There are large areas of trees that surround the entire structure and a formal garden in which the house is harmoniously inserted. Seemingly English in the romantic style, the garden has numerous flowers and fascinating details. The fountains and paths, the carved benches and stone tables invite one to stop and contemplate the surroundings. With centennial trees and exotic plants, hedges, and bushes, and the lakes and fountains as water features, this garden feels like stepping into a fantasy. Numerous small houses around the garden—such as the ducks' or the goats' houses—add to the fairytale setting.

The house has two large turrets and a central body, with the charming ivy-covered façades. Inside, the house unfolds into several worlds giving one an almost cinematic experience walking through, enhanced by details such as the collection of ceramics from Caldas da Rainha are displayed on the ceiling. There are numerous wallpapers, prints, textures, and colors, blended in an organized manner that shows the personality of the family. Each room is a microcosm, each with its own matching wallpaper, bedspread, and lampshades. One feels the urge to stop, look closely, and discover another new detail. The living room is furnished with antique pieces and hand-painted wallpaper. Family photographs litter the house, some still in their original rococo style porcelain frames.

Of all the houses we visited, this is one of the most sophisticated. From the interiors to the gardens—all in a grand scale—it is sensorially rich in decorative elements and details.

VII

Casa em Caxias

THIS LATE 17TH CENTURY farmhouse, which has served as a retirement home for the Charterhouse of Caxias, is a relatively short drive from the center of Lisbon.

Outside, the charming garden is accented with 17th- and 18th-century tiles used on both a tank and a fountain—classic Portuguese elements. It is all well-preserved and matches other panels of the same pattern found inside the house. The interior tiles from the 18th century are decorated with individual figures and cover the walls of the kitchen, which is packed with copper utensils and traditional Portuguese ceramic wares, and with copper pans and ceramics hanging from the celings.

Walking through the other rooms, one is impressed by a myriad of delightful collections such as vintage clay figurines from the Estremoz area of Alentejo; beautiful glass bottles of various shapes, colors, and origins; religious relics; rare 19th-century *Ratinho* faience plates from Coimbra; crystals; and many other treasures. The house also hosts a collection of Portuguese paintings, prominently featuring several works by Milly Possoz (1888–1968), a prominent figure of the first generation of modernist artists in Portugal.

These special decorative elements embody so many memories and give life and significance to the house.

Amo-te muito

AVESSA

VIII

Quinta do Vesúvio

SET IN A UNIQUE LANDSCAPE that is specific to Douro, visiting Quinta do Vesúvio is an adventure. Wedged between the overwhelming landscape of the Douro Valley and the scenic train line that follows along the river, this isolated property is a true monument to times gone by.

It is considered the favorite property of Antónia Adelaide Ferreira, the matriarch who left a mark on the wine history of the Douro. When she took over the administration of *Casa* Ferreirinha in 1844, she commissioned improvements to the house and chapel. Entering the house, one immediately feels a feminine atmosphere thanks to a profusion of small details such as the cushions under the windows or the frills that fall under the curtains.

Inspired by the baroque style, it has a "U" layout consisting of two longitudinal two-story bodies (the north façade ends up having one more due to the necessary compensation caused by the slope of the valley) joined by a transversal wing. It has an impressive twenty-three rooms, all of them decorated in a sober manner. Each has its own palette and an organization system that is always identical, only the background color of the fabrics changes. The fabrics are Alcobaça chintz and the color is repeated in the cushions, chairs, curtains, bedspreads, and even in the structures that make up the closets.

One of the most impressive details of this house is its neo-baroque chapel. With a façade facing the Douro that stands out for its special sobriety and elegance, it benefits from incredible natural light. Its interior are mostly granite and walls covered in traditional blue and white tiles with revivalist patterns of the 19th century.

This estate has a strong connection with the territory—the vineyard more specifically, but also with the hills that surround the property—so much so that António Bernardo Ferreira who founded the property in 1823 named this piece of land after the Neapolitan volcano. Such were the similarities he saw between this Italian icon and a specific hill that can be seen from the house.

QUINTA DO VESUVIO
1
20571

IX

Casa Branca

ALONE ON A CLIFF in Azenhas do Mar next to the Atlantic Ocean stands a house designed by the epic Portuguese architect Raul Lino to spend his holidays near Lisbon. Finalized in 1920, Casa Branca (White House) is an iconic landmark. It is impossible to pass by it without wondering about its history and feeling curious about its interiors. Simplicity is the best way to describe it. Ultimately, it is Lino's erudite reinterpretation of the popular housing of the fishermen and farmers of this area.

This relatively small house is whitewashed and has charming wood shutters painted orange. It opens onto the ocean through a dreamy main door that hides on the ground floor, a living room, a small kitchen with a log-burning oven in a corner, and a bedroom.

Recently celebrating 100 years, it is impeccably well maintained and remains faithful to its origins. The floor is composed of rustic tiles, the interior walls are whitewashed with a thin blue stripe, and its crockery includes several traditional Portuguese ceramic plates. Walking through the divisions feels like sailing through a time capsule, emphasized further in that it has no electricity or running water.

The top floor is a comfortable space of rest flooded with natural light, nature, and breathtaking views of the ocean. The two bedrooms found on this level are furnished with items from the Alentejo region of Portugal, made and painted by hand. The bedspreads and curtains are made of Alcobaça chintz, a decorative element that we found in many of the houses we visited.

This home is raw beauty and would be a marvelous place to spend a balmy summer day or a soul enriching stormy night.

1754
1754
MOFINA
MENDES
ALCOBAÇA
AGOSTO
1941
CASTRO
ALCOBAÇA
AGOSTO
1941

1849

X

Palácio Sousa da Câmara

WE RETURN TO ALENTEJO to visit another unique property, this time in Vila Viçosa in the Évora district. It is here where we find the Sousa da Câmara Palace in the historic town center. This house, which has been in the same family's possession for 300 years, is a paradise for any mural painting enthusiast. The house was designed by the architect José Francisco de Abreu who was the author of other civil and religious buildings in the village. Since the '50s, this palace has been divided into two parts for two different branches of the family. We visited and photographed the Morais Sarmento side.

Despite the grandeur and its long history, this palace exudes a certain lightness which is very special. This is noticeable straightaway at the entrance as one crosses a typical Alentejo courtyard with arcades, whitewashed walls, and a stone floor decorated with potted plants. This sensation continues as one follows some stairs through several mysterious vaults until you reach a succession of rooms that are interconnected in a fluid and very elegant way. In the game, reading, and dining rooms there are a series of murals that create a unique atmosphere, where patterns mix with floral elements and figurative representations, providing an unexpected visual experience full of personality.

The interiors of Casa Sousa da Câmara are distinguished by these murals that cover most of the rooms. A variety of neoclassic motifs are allied with good taste and careful decorating skills. This symbiotic relationship is seen in the living room where the mural painting is detailed and erudite. It covers the walls and ceiling in lines of garlands and chains with vegetable and floral designs in warm colors that combine perfectly with the golden-brown velvet sofas, the frames around the paintings, and the curtains. Equally rich is the dining room with a variety of decorative elements inspired by the classic grotesque. Winged pairs emerge from cornucopias linked by crowns of flowers and bowls and urns framed by groupings of leaves. In the corner of the room, small marble shelves exhibit high-quality porcelain pieces. The built-in cabinet painted green keeps the dishware and everyday glasses.

The kitchen—which is always one of the most interesting places—is simpler, reminiscent of the ones that existed in old Portuguese country houses, with a rustic brick ceiling supported by sturdy wooden beams. Here, both wood and tiles coexist harmoniously, creating an aesthetic of a certain purity and chromatic simplicity that does not lose its power when compared to the many greens and yellows that decorate the palace.

There is an aura of sober elegance, a prevailing sentiment that makes us want to spend as much time as possible within these walls.

33

XI

Quinta das Areias

FOR A HOUSE that was designed over a century ago, Quinta das Areias, located north of Lisbon in Vila Franca de Xira, is an audacious and unexpected build. The family who owns the house shared the unique story of its past with us. Their great-great-grandfather José Pereira Palha Blanco (1854–1937) fell in love with some architectural watercolors that he saw when he visited the 1889 Paris Exhibition for which the Eiffel Tower was built. He was so enamored by them that he brought the drawings to Portugal and commissioned an exact replica be made, a far cry from what was the Portuguese architectural style of that time.

As one approaches its entrance, the immensity of the place is striking. A daring puzzle of materials and patterns somehow fit together harmoniously. All the rooms have stoneware flooring with complex geometric patterns in different colors that coexist with imposing wooden ceilings, screens, wallpapers, and tile panels. This bold composition between decorative elements is greatly enhanced by the soft, playful natural light.

The dining room stands out, with its walls covered in fabric with plant motifs, exuberant ceiling of wood panels, and the sideboards and cupboards made of solid oak with bronze bas-reliefs. There is a small, in comparison to the size of the home, chapel on the grounds that is in impeccable condition. Mass is still held there every Sunday for family and friends.

Quinta das Areias has a creative atmosphere and feels cherished by the different generations that have lived in it. Our lunch in the lush garden allowed us to fantasize and wonder about the history of this property and the many characters that had walked through these impressive rooms.

A. Rey Colaço

XII

Quinta da Fonte do Anjo

LIKE ANY EUROPEAN capital after the industrial revolution, Lisbon has seen its size multiply with many of its periphery areas transformed to house the ever-growing population and industry. There is something exquisitely exciting about discovering a house like this in the busy Lisbon area of Olivais, an area where urban planning has taken a more functional aspect. This property, built over two hundred years ago, still stands—partially hidden—as a living testament to a time of more inspirational architecture. Passing through its imposing façade we immediately forget our surroundings full of practical modern buildings.

The chapel stands out, its silhouette so large it looks more like a church. Its ceilings worked in the style of Giovanni Grossi (1715–1780) are stunning, as are the wall paintings. The house itself is packed with many impressive decorative features and aesthetically pleasing details that evoke a poetic flare. It is surrounded by charming gardens, one of them with beautiful boxwood.

The walls are covered with murals attributed to the famous French painter Jean Baptiste Pillement (1728–1808) and Portuguese tile panels with various designs from the 18th century. There is a feminine aura in the air, a calm romanticism that remains untouched even after the renovations that began at the turn of the 19th century. One of the rooms with paintings in the neoclassical revivalist style, for example, dates from this period as do the coffered ceilings, the fireplace, and the marbled stucco paneling in the entrance hall.

We were lucky to spend time with one of the owners who generously shared many memories that increased our curiosity. The home abounds in nature, art, and history.

XIII

Casa e Quinta dos Condes de Carnide

WE COULD NOT IMAGINE that behind the green doors was not only a 18th-century palace but also a vast garden and an alley of centenary olive trees, right in the north outskirts of Lisbon. When it was built, the Casa e Quinta dos Condes de Carnide was a farmhouse outside the city but as Lisbon, but as the city grew it became an urban treasure within the city proper. As soon as the green doors closed behind us, we were surprised by the silence. The ambient noise of the city disappeared, filled instead by the lullaby and scents of nature.

In the *Pombalino*-style house, you can see the various interventions that the property has undergone. A fire in the 1900s almost destroyed it entirely. The interiors, with very high ceilings are all connected, each more beautiful than the next, leading to a boxwood garden that is accessible via a monumental baroque staircase covered with impressive and unique 18th-century tiles.

The living rooms on the first floor are decorated with stucco and frescoes that are in excellent condition thanks to a recent restoration. However, they also feature original 18th-century tile panels. You can sense the historical and emotional significance of this property as you look at the objects decorating the rooms—the photographs, paintings, and books that adorn each division. Our favorite space was the blue kitchen and its large, tiled walls decorated with a collection of antique copper pans and yellow armchairs that suggest a place of contemplation and slower moments peppered with conversation and family memories.

SABER ESCOLHER
SABER ESCOLHER
As Melhores Receitas de Claudia

AÇUCAR
FEIJÃO
MASSA
CAFÉ

XIV

Casa de Santiago

ON ONE SIDE, the Beja Cathedral, on the other an imposing section of the wall that served as defense of this city in Alentejo, and in the middle you will find Casa de Santiago, a very notable mansion dating to the 18th century. The façade is sober and elegant. The main floor features four windows and just above the roof you can see the two-octagonal chimneys. When we walked through the door what immediately stood out was the immense arches in the ceiling with exposed brick, a vernacular element of this region's architectural culture.

A multitude of generous details accent nearly every element of the house—from the guardrail of the impressive stone staircase that features an animal head at the end to the small stars painted on the ceiling. There is a magical and unexpected feel to everything. You never know what new little accent you will stumble upon.

The stateroom houses one of the most impressive decorative elements, a set of mural panels, which set a decorative tone. They allude to the sea, each panel with a monumental grisaille frame with architectural motifs of baroque inspiration. Shells, caryatids touching conches from which small starfish emerge, and, on the smaller walls, a ribbon formed by small shells and bows decorated with coral crowns carry the sea theme into the house. The paintings are completed at the bottom with a painting of a Greek figure with birds and garlands of neoclassical inspiration. The stateroom is capped with an oak coffered ceiling dating to 19th century. In the next room, the pictorial theme refers to earthly environments with emphasis on a boxwood garden with a fountain. One of the panels demonstrates a gallant scene, another an open-air dance. The panels are finished by a painting of an azulejo tile in *trompe l'oeil* bordered by Corinthian columns. The valances above the doors are also painted in *trompe l'oeil*. The exceptional nature of these highly decorative paintings is the result of the free interpretation of erudite themes, using tiles and engravings as sources of iconographic and compositional inspiration, combined with more popular ones.

The beautiful parquet work of the flooring is also unavoidable, as are the details on the ironwork. The house has numerous beautiful handrails and railings that carry out onto the balcony. The sophistication of this work shows a special eye and care for detail that was taken at every turn in this house.

MOBILIÁRIO PORTUGUÊS
MOBILIÁRIO PORTUGUÊS
MOBILIÁRIO PORTUGUÊS

XV

Villa Roma

ON THE DAY we visited Villa Roma, we were welcomed with Sintra's classic cloudy weather that only served to further accentuate the charm of this place. As soon as we crossed the gate, we were confronted with an imposing façade of plaster imitating brick, an Anglophile inspiration that denoted Italian neoclassic influence and highlighted the romantic architectural trend of the 19th century.

This excellent example of the romantic period, which is neighbor to Quinta da Regaleira and Quinta do Relógio, was designed by the architect António Manuel da Fonseca (1796–1879) in 1856 and remained in the original owner's family to this day. This sense of strong family heritage and respect for tradition is felt through the pieces of period furniture that give the space an intimate, elegant, and comforting touch.

The garden, full of centennial trees that serve as a frame for the village of Sintra which can be seen in the distance. This exquisite garden is seen from the large windows of the rooms with parquet floors and light shades of green and pink, which add lightness to the space. However, it is the beautiful frescoes with floral and geometric motifs that decorate the walls that are most treasured and add an air of elegance to the home.

It was a romantic trip and home, learning the history of this family who generously opened their doors to us.

BIOGRAPHIES

AUTHORS

Ana Anahory

Ana Anahory, born in Lisbon in 1982, is an architect and interior designer. After completing her architecture degree, including a senior year in Rome in 2005, she returned to Portugal to collaborate with her architect father. During this period, she worked on various projects while developing her own practice, focusing on restaurants and private residences.

In 2011, Ana co-founded the AnahoryAlmeida Studio with Felipa Almeida. Over nine years, they designed numerous hospitality and interior architecture projects, including restaurants for Chef José Avillez and the Hotel São Lourenço do Barrocal. Their work emphasized Portuguese materials and involved collaborations with local artists and artisans. In 2020, they decided to close the studio to pursue individual ambitions.

Since then, Ana has focused on Estúdio Lisboa, a project she previously founded with her husband, José António Uva, where she leads the interior design team. Estúdio Lisboa develops hospitality projects in Portugal, offering services from conception and architecture to design and operations management. Each project highlights a sense of place, working with Portuguese materials and craft techniques in collaboration with local artisans, resulting in timeless and simple designs.

Felipa Almeida

Felipa Almeida (b. 1979), is a curator and art director specializing in the intersection of art, crafts, and Portugal's material culture and traditions. With degrees in Art History and Curatorial Studies, Felipa's work celebrates and preserves Portuguese heritage.

Returning to Portugal in 2006, she joined the architect Ana Anahory to open the architecture and interior design studio AnahoryAlmeida (2011–2020) which focused on working with Portuguese materials. It was during this defining period that Felipa started collaborating closely with artists and craftspeople whose work became part of the spaces developed in the studio. AnahoryAlmeida Studio designed numerous hospitality and interior architecture projects including São Lourenço do Barrocal Hotel, Quinta das Murças House, and chef José Avillez's restaurants in Lisbon.

In 2020 she established a creative studio in Lisbon where she collaborates with artists and artisans. She curates exhibitions, bespoke projects and collections, and promotes themed pop-ups challenging artists to create unique pieces on a specific theme. Since 2024 she has worked with Estudio Alhures to edit and publish books about Portuguese crafts and private folk-art collections.

CONTRIBUTORS

BIRGIT SFAT

Birgit Sfat (b. 1974), is a photographer and creative consultant based in Lisbon. Her passion for photography and for Portugal developed naturally—both her parents were photographers, and since the early 1990s, she spent time each year at the family home near Tavira.

After studying economics, Birgit worked as a strategist in Munich, helping shape collections, communication, and brand identity for fashion labels before moving to San Francisco with her husband and daughter. There, she founded Over the Ocean, which reflected her interest in thoughtful design, storytelling, and the work of small European makers. In 2019, the family relocated to Portugal permanently and settled in Lisbon.

Birgit's work explores spaces, objects, and atmospheres—often at the intersection of personal memory and cultural heritage. With a clear, intuitive eye, she seeks out the quiet stories within interiors, capturing textures, light, and details that convey a sense of presence and place. Her photography is rooted in observation and simplicity, with a focus on interiors, travel, and portraiture. Her images have been featured in international magazines such as Milk Magazine and Journal Voyageurs, and in the book Family Adventures (Gestalten, 2021).

FILIPA AVELLAR

Filipa Avellar was born in Lisbon in 1961 and has a deep passion for Portuguese history and art. She holds a degree in Historical Sciences (1984) and a Master's in Paleography and Diplomatics (1996) from the Faculty of Arts and Humanities of the University of Lisbon. For twenty years, she taught at the History Department of Universidade Lusíada, where she found fulfilment in sharing her knowledge.

From 2001 to 2007, she was invited by the Directorate-General for National Buildings and Monuments to coordinate the Portuguese Epigraphy section of the Architectural Heritage Inventory. This role took her across Portugal, allowing her to experience the country's heritage from a broader perspective while deepening her admiration for it.

Currently, Filipa dedicates herself to organizing courses, lectures, and cultural tours to promote Portuguese history and art, both domestically and internationally. Her goal is to inspire pride in being Portuguese and to foster a deeper appreciation for the nation's cultural legacy.

ACKNOWLEDGMENTS

This book is a homage to Portuguese houses and the families that, with effort and love, preserve them through time. It is with immense gratitude that we thank those for permitting us entry into their homes, their memories, and to capture a little bit of the intimacy shared within and family traditions. Thank you, from the bottom of our hearts. This book would not have happened without you.

Thank you, Martinho Pimentel from Casa do Cipreste, Maria do Carmo Martins Pereira from Casa Leal, Sampaio da Nóvoa family from Quinta de Boamense, Lupi Cary family from Quinta das Gaeiras, Frederico and João Melo Franco from Casa Sebastião, the Guedes family from Quinta da Aveleda, Anne and Friquette Demoustier from House in Caxias, the Symington family from Quinta do Vesúvio, Ana and Bernardo Almada Pimentel from Casa Branca, the Sousa da Câmara family from Palácio Sousa da Câmara, Legatees of José Pereira Palha Blanco from Casa da Quinta das Areias, the Amorim Ferreira family from Quinta da Fonte do Anjo, Joana Mayer and Alexandre Carnide from Casa e Quinta dos Condes de Carnide, the Vilhena Freire de Andrade family from Casa de Santiago, and Miguel Oliveira and Carlos Matos from Villa Roma.

Thank you to António Ribeiro Telles Costa for your valuable insight shared with Filipa Avellar about Casa da Quinta das Areias, to Roberto Guedes for the same with Quinta da Aveleda, and to Frederico Melo Franco for the text about Casa São Sebastião.

We are particularly thankful to Birgit Sfat, our dear photographer, who without hesitation accepted our challenge to photograph fifteen Portuguese houses with the goal of capturing the souls of these houses with an open heart.

We are also grateful to Filipa Avellar, who enthusiastically helped us find some of the houses, helped provide contact with the families, and provided historical context for each house.

Thank you to Diogo Lopes for editing all the text. Thank you to Rita Sevilha for helping us express in writing our feelings when we visited the houses. Thank you Rosa Mello do Rego for the subtle tweaks to the English text.

Lastly, thank you to ORO Editions for believing in this book.